A Land Of Kebab
And Curries

Aisha Idris Suleman

BookLeaf Publishing

India | USA | UK

Presentation by *BookLeaf Publishing*

Web: www.bookleafpub.com

E-mail: info@bookleafpub.com

ISBN: 978-93-5761-240-1

First edition 2022

DEDICATION

This book is gratefully dedicated to my four-year-old son, who taught me to live my life joyfully and freely. I would also like to dedicate this book once again to my late father (1956 - 2020), who trained me to face challenges that may arise and live my dreams to the fullest.

I affectionately dedicate this book to all my wonderful readers, as well as to all those who think they are alone, may you find happiness, courage and peace. I love you all!

ACKNOWLEDGEMENT

The world is a better place when people want to develop and motivate others by helping them to reach their greatest potential. I want to thank every person that shares the gift of their time by striving to motivate others.

To all the individuals I have had the opportunity to motivate, be motivated by or watch their motivation from a great distance; I thank you from the bottom of my heart for being the inspiration and foundation of this book.

I want to thank all my beautiful readers and fans for making this dream of mine come true. Writing a compilation of poetry and converting it into a book is both challenging and difficult, but the experience is rewarding.

Most of all, I want to thank BookLeaf Publishing for showcasing my talent to the world yet again, as well as publishing my second book!

PREFACE

Most of the poems in this book have been written from my own personal experiences, which I encountered throughout my life so far. I have mentioned in my previous book how I see poetry as a form of therapy, as it helps me to express how I feel, since I can find it difficult at times to explain what is going through my mind. Though I like to write poems on various subjects that are currently circulating in the world, I also feel it is helpful to share some of my own experiences, as there could be people out there that may be on the same boat as me and going through similar situations or have been through hard times, but feel anxious to share it with anyone.

Giving and touching other's lives has always been one of my core values and the aim of this poetry book is the same. I know there are many people out there in the world that struggle to express how they feel or are not able to show who they really are because they fear about the remarks that they may receive. No two human beings are the same, but I enjoy encouraging people through my poems, so that they can get the best of life and live it the way they would like to live it. When I write straight from my heart, the words come along naturally and a beautiful piece is achieved. This can be a bit daunting, but at the same time, it can be hugely rewarding.

I have not had the best childhood experience and was fearful of my mother because of her controlling behaviour and beatings. She would never let me live my life the way I wanted to live it and never understood what I wanted, until I started taking a stand for myself and speaking up fearlessly. It is my father who always picked me up, directed me towards my goals and stood by me in every situation. As you read through my poems in this book, you will notice how I have mentioned him greatly because he has always been my true hero from the day I was born. Though he is not with me in this world, I know he is watching over me and he must be so proud of who I am today.

Most of the poems in this book are my own short stories in the form of poetry, which I truly hope will touch your heart and empower those that are struggling to express themselves or take steps, which they feel are right for them. Remember, you are in control of your destiny, so

be fearless and release yourself in A Land Of
Kebab And Curries!

Challenges

Life is full of challenges
Good, bad or even savages
Hard to deal with at times
Similar to wailing of chimes

Some trials are there to push
Helping you to come out of the bush
Making you realise your inner soul
One that maybe you could not control

Challenges can be a real surprise
Never imagined till you open your eyes
No need to back off or fear
Alone you stand with nobody near

Stand up with real confidence
There is no need for any evidence
Face those hurdles and tests
Strapped with bullet proof vests

However difficult the challenge
Don't lose your balance
The road may be endless
But never feel defenceless!

Change The Narrow Thinking

Welcome to the twenty-first century

Let's make this poem into a good memory

I have plenty of motivation and energy

The narrow thinking needs to alter, come and
follow me

Stop with the forced marriages

Sending your daughters in beautiful carriages

Without asking for their consent

Coercing them to smile throughout the event

Lesbian, Gay, Bisexual or Queer

There is no need to be shy or fear

Love is love and it will remain

There is no need for you to explain

What is the point of racism and hatred?

Religion or ethnicity does not make things
complicated

No need to thread people according to these
groups

We are all equal, so stop forming these troops

Treating children like they did in the back days

Influencing them in their old fashioned ways

End this kind of torture and mentality

Please wake up to the current reality

Why distinguish between a man and woman?

That is just utterly inhumane

Both sexes can undertake any form of work

Stop prioritising and being a jerk

No child should ever suffer

Black lives will always matter

Palestinians are no different to any other

I hope you will soon discover!

A Year Has Passed

How the year has passed
Time is just going so fast
But I still feel your presence
As well as your beautiful essence

You are always on my mind
You left your belongings behind
I hug them close to my heart
As if it is you, though we are far apart

Not a single day goes by
When I look up at the sky
Praying that you are safe and well
You could read me without me having to tell

The life lessons you have taught
Are something I have not forgot
I am on cloud nine, with achievements and fame
Thanks to you father, I wholeheartedly use your
name

Your death can never be forgotten
My tears cannot be wiped with tissue or cotton
But then I look at my reflection in the fresh
water

Reminding myself, I am AISHA IDRIS
SULEMAN, your princess and daughter!

6

Beaten

A cute and innocent child

So adorable and mild

Was beaten by her mother

Which she kept hidden

Under the duvet cover

For the littlest mistakes

Which all kids make

Would be like torture

Similar to a day of scorcher

What is the need?

For such an evil deed

Mothers are usually caring

Not harsh and blaring

Those slaps and pinches

Like wild cats counting inches

So painful and endless

Making childhood feel reckless

But father was the hero

Counting down to zero

Always cuddling his princess

Guiding her the route to success

Never raised his hand

Always took her stand

Kissing her forehead

Putting her to sleep

In her cosy bed

Waking up one morning

Seeing the new day dawning

Feeling so strong and grown up

Holding wonder like a glittery cup

Head high and soul sturdy

No more caged like a birdie

Not taking any more crap

Nor living in mother's trap!

Father

Why did you leave me?
The worst tragedy that can be
You were always by my side
It feels like there is no place to hide

You used to fill me with sunshine
Because you were always mine
Our bonding was like no other
Not the one you had with my sister or brother

Life feels empty without you
My heart feels tangled up in blue
Seems like you are watching me from heaven
Whether it is five o'clock or ten to seven

I miss you from top to bottom
You are a charm that can never be forgotten
I wish I could feel your presence
All your belongings are quiescent

I will always be your princess
Wearing your favourite dress
Making the world a better place
With a beautiful smile on my face

Father, you are my best friend
Your death is not the end
You are still the rock I look up to
Following the footprints left by you!

Never Loved You

I never loved you
Being honest and true
I was forcibly tied
So I had to abide

You were not my sort
So I took you to court
Your true colours came out
Without me having to shout

Though we felt rumpy-pumpy once
I utterly found you to be a dunce
For which I paid the price for
Thanks to my mother for sure

A signature on a piece of paper
Does not mean I will love you later
Those feelings were always missing
Regardless of the lustful texts and kissing

You were never in my heart
Very right from the start
I was eager to leave you
Because life just felt so blue!

Freedom

I love to open my wings and be free
Be as happy as I can possibly be
Leaving the sorrows and fears behind
Making it exclusively difficult to find

I am not into marriages or tied relationships
Though I still enjoy a kiss on my delicate lips
I don't like being controlled or dominated
It makes me feel severely incriminated

I like to explore and be innovative
Multi-task and be extremely creative
Enjoying all the aspects of this life
Expunging all the heartaches and strife

Freedom is the key to happiness
With a sweet touch of tenderness
I will continue to spread my wings
Giving this world my unique encolourings!

Tomorrow

When life puts her down
And she has a huge frown
She does not run and hide
She buries her feelings inside.

Her heart feels heavy
It feels like a Chevy
The world seems dark
Like the belly of a shark.

These awful mind games
Are shooting her down in flames
Without a shadow of doubt
She really needs to get out!

Stop thinking about the past
Because tomorrow is coming fast
Her voice was low in pain
She was treated like a dog on a chain.

How can one be evil?
Harming others like a little weevil
They forget tomorrow will come
And shock them with sour and glum.

Her soul tells her to fight
Because she is very bright
What is there to fear?
When God is always near.

She looks up at the blue sky
So beautiful and high
As each day goes by
She sees the light shining in her eye.

Why shall she be sad?
She cannot separate the good from bad
There is a beautiful life ahead
That is strung together on a thread.

She wants to be happy
With her cute little chappie
Cradling him in her arms
Because he is one of her luck charms.

She does not want to waste time
The road is a long hard climb
Before she reaches tomorrow
Leaving behind the bag full of sorrow!

Single

Being single is my game
It gives me so much fame
No arguments or blames
Or calling out dirty names

I am a good flirt
That is truly overt
Wearing a beautiful skirt
With my stunning red shirt

Not tied up with anyone
Just have one gorgeous son
Enjoying life and having fun
Not thinking about what is done

Feels like I am sweet sixteen
I am here and there, always seen
Getting attention like the queen
Whether I wear red, pink or green!

Memories

Memories are to treasure
Bringing back blossom with pleasure
Regardless of the good or sad
It is the preeminent you ever had

Memories are like an album
Similar to that of platinum
Looking at what you went through
Visioning what you can do

Some memories are permanently wiped out
Don't want to tell anyone what it was about
No need to keep them stored in
Just discard them in the loony bin

Let your memories unfold
And hasten for the old
You can't live them again
But you can simply pretend!

Enjoying Life

Always loved my freedom
Whatever the month or season
Sharing myself with everyone
Having full on pleasure and fun

Giving and receiving love
On cloud nine, so high above
Always being the popular one
Similar to the yellow flashing sun

My presence is never forgotten
In every person's heart like cotton
Giving attention and spreading joy
Somewhat all souls wish to employ

Always chatty and playful
And people are so grateful
For having me in their lives
The one that always strives

So come and join my frisky world
You will feel relaxed and unfurled
Forgetting all your stress and sorrows
I am here to fill your todays and tomorrows!

Voice For The Voiceless

Voice for the voiceless

That is totally priceless

Scream, shout and yell

And get my poems to spell

The issues faced in the current society

Causing so much fear and anxiety

Whether it is Free Palestine or Black Lives Matter

Hatred and racism will make our world shatter

The knives and killing must be put to an end

Why can't we all just be each other's friend?

Our lives will be less complicated and stressful

I am going to get my points across and be helpful

Enough is enough, stop pointing out differences

Black, White or Asian, we have our unique appearances

Lesbian, gay or bisexual, no need to be shy

You were born to survive, so no need to cry

It does not matter what your religion or culture

We should stand side by side, similar to carved sculpture

Wherever you go and whatever you do, spread joy, love and peace

So join me and help hatred, racism and crime to cease!

Dedicated To You…

Let me thank all the famous writers around the
world
Who have inspired me to get hold of my pen and
notebook
Without them, my mind would have just whirled
Making me feel like an old pothook.

I enjoy delving into the writing of many famous
people
From the well-known Robert Hayden to Emily
Dickinson
These are just a few names to scribble
There are many more, which are yet to come.

William Wordsworth was well-known for
romanticism
The Excursion, An Evening Walk and Lyrical
Ballads are some famous pieces
All of which are extremely awesome
And have helped me with my knowledge by
filling gaps and connecting bridges.

Poems about the natural world are a great genre
Robert Frost taught that nature can teach
something about ourselves

A fierce animal could express wilder human
glimpse
So I was tempted to pick nature books off the
library shelf.

I honour all the famous writers out there
That gave me the courage to write write write
I will continue to brighten the world with my
unique flare
Until there are more people that can gain an
insight!

Act of Kindness

Be kind to everyone around you
Avoiding hatred and making lives blue
It will make you feel so much better
Feeding the poor or writing someone an
encouraging letter

There are so many ways to spread love
Through a bunch of flowers or gifting someone
with warm gloves
Leave an impression that would make people
happy
Not one that would make people feel mad or
scrappy

The world is craving for peace and kindness
But hatred and fights have caused human
blindness
Let's remove this tight blindfold together
So that we can live peacefully forever!

Express Yourself

Let yourself open up
Go on, break that cup
Show me how you feel
And I will make you heal

Don't keep it stored in
Or you will never win
Look yourself in the eye
Let me help you reach the sky

What is keeping you curled?
Understand this is a free world
Where you cannot be controlled
As you are not a product sold

Let me dig into you
And see why you are blue
Come into my world
Where you will never be hurled

Grab my arms firmly
So we can start our journey
There is no need to be shy
Because I promise you will fly!

It's Your Birthday Dad – 30 December

It's your birthday Dad
But I am feeling sad
Because you are not here
For whom I party and cheer

You love your chocolate cake
As well as some chips with steak
Always looking forward to your gifts
Your lovely smile automatically lifts

Today just feels so empty
I was looking forward to plenty
I am aching from the inside
This feeling, I can just not hide

I will still celebrate your birthday
This time, in a different way
Feeding the poor, helping the needy
Your princess has a big heart, not greedy

You come into my dreams
You are in a safe place it seems

Always happy and smiling
Like a beautiful star shining

So, happy birthday my hero
Without you, my life feels zero
Not forgetting I am your daughter, your princess
One that strives to be number one and gain
success!

Diamond

You shine like a diamond

Precious and unique on the island

Eyes cannot stop gazing

You are just so amazing

Feeling so energetic and free

Seems like you were waiting for me

Picturing you in the blue sky

Gosh you make me feel so high

Imagine two diamonds in the twilight

Glimmering like the watery moonlight

All facing towards our presence

Behold the delightful essence

You stand out from the crowd

Similar to a precious emerald

Words are not enough to describe

How good it feels from the inside

So continue being the brightest diamond

Not complicated like a hexiamond

Whether you are near or distant

Bumping into each other will be consistent!

Age

Age is defined as a number
Old and fit, even if others slumber
Wrinkly and crinkly is what they see
The heart may still be young and free

Nothing can stop you from having fun
Dancing, singing or bathing in the sun
Even running a 26.2 miles marathon
No need to be shy, you are still number one

Live life to the fullest regardless of age
Your book flowing with every different page
No need to feel isolated in that cage
A number cannot stop you from performing on
stage

Falling in love with someone young
Lips moving until the songs are sung
Ethnicity and sexuality may cause strife
Not letting anyone obstruct your life

Inside out, your beauty will remain
Regardless of health conditions and pain
Don't let numbers define your health and fitness
Just be you and tell them to mind their business!

Who Is She?

The way she walks…

The way she talks…

The way she stares…

Looks like she cares…

Is there a way out?...

What is all this about?...

Let's have some grilled trout…

With a tablespoon of beansprout…

I know her name…

But I want to play this game…

Not put her to shame…

But give her a bit of fame…

Why do we bump into each other?...

I really want to discover…

No words to utter…

Just a silent gaze and flutter…

We are near but distant…

Why is it consistent?...

Why such a narrow-minded resistance?...

Probably special moments, but not sufficient…

Is she hiding something?...

Her eyes are so touching…

Maybe a dream that I was hunting…

Not sure, let me just continue munching!!!

The New Year

The New Year is finally here
A new beginning with some cheer
Happiness may be down the road
Hang in there, it will gradually unfold

Stay positive and keep that smile
Some things can just take a while
Amazing surprises and SMART goals
All of which will touch our souls

So much to look forward to
Keep that spirit, it will come true
We are all in this battle together
The world will ultimately become better

So 2022, bring us some joy
There is nothing more left to destroy
Fill our lives with laughter and fun
That is easier said than done!

Escape

Hold my hand and let us escape
Don't look around, just wear your cape
There is so much to see in the outer world
No need to stay at home all curled

Beautiful greenery and the sound of ducks
Focus properly and hear my tender words
Children running and adults socialising
The lockdown is over, this is hardly surprising

Let's dance in the park or sing in the woods
Make this quiet place into a lively
neighbourhood
No thinking, just living each moment to the
fullest
Not letting anyone control and fire their bullet

Watch the birds fly above the blue sky
The sun beams glimmering so high
Tall trees swaying in the cool breeze
Enjoy every minute and put your mind at ease

An escape is sometimes all we need
Foot off the accelerator to reduce the speed

Giving our bodies and mind a good break
Imagine the difference that would make!

34